STRONG KIDS HEALTHY PLATE

Powerful Proteins

Katie Marsico

CHERRY LAKE PRESS

Published in the United States of America
by Cherry Lake Publishing Group
Ann Arbor, Michigan
www.cherrylakepublishing.com

Content Adviser: Debbie Fetter, PhD, Assistant Professor of Teaching Nutrition, University of California, Davis
Reading Adviser: Marla Conn, MS, Ed., Literacy specialist, Read-Ability, Inc.

Photo Credits: ©Andrea and Paul Renshaw/Shutterstock.com, front cover; ©baibaz/Shutterstock.com, 1; ©Viktor Kochetkov/Shutterstock.com, 4; ©LightFiel Studios/Shutterstock.com, 6; ©Ekaterina Markelova/Shutterstock.com, 8; Kasabutskaya Nataliya/Shutterstock.com, 10; ©USDA/ChooseMyPlate.gov, 12; ©Anatoliy Karlyuk/Shutterstock.com, 14; ©Ann in the UK/Shutterstock.com, 16; ©MSPhotographic/Shutterstock.com, 18; ©Nutria3000/Shutterstock.com, 20

Copyright @2021 by Cherry Lake Publishing Group
All rights reserved. No part of this book may be reproduced or utilized in any form or by any means without written permission from the publisher.

Cherry Lake Press is an imprint of Cherry Lake Publishing Group.

Library of Congress Cataloging-in-Publication Data

Names: Marsico, Katie, 1980- author.
Title: Powerful proteins / written by Katie Marsico.
Description: Ann Arbor, Michigan : Cherry Lake Publishing, 2020. | Series: 21st century basic skills library. Level 3 | Includes index. | Audience: Grades K-1 | Summary: "Proteins helps your body's cells work, but did you know your body can't make protein on its own? Discover tasty protein food choices to help you grow and maintain a healthy diet. Content encourages balance and making healthy choices. This level 3 guided reader is based on the U.S. government's diet recommendations. Readers will develop word recognition and reading skills while learning about food and where it comes from. Includes table of contents, glossary, index, author biographies, and word list for home and school connection"— Provided by publisher.
Identifiers: LCCN 2020002797 (print) | LCCN 2020002798 (ebook) | ISBN 9781534168657 (hardcover) | ISBN 9781534170339 (paperback) | ISBN 9781534172173 (pdf) | ISBN 9781534174016 (ebook)
Subjects: LCSH: Proteins in human nutrition—Juvenile literature. | Food—Protein content—Juvenile literature.
Classification: LCC TX553.P7 M367 2020 (print) | LCC TX553.P7 (ebook) | DDC 613.2/82—dc23
LC record available at https://lccn.loc.gov/2020002797
LC ebook record available at https://lccn.loc.gov/2020002798

Cherry Lake Publishing Group would like to acknowledge the work of the Partnership for 21st Century Learning, a Network of Battelle for Kids. Please visit http://www.battelleforkids.org/networks/p21 for more information.

Printed in the United States of America
Corporate Graphics

Table of Contents

5   What Are Protein Foods?
13   An Important Part of Your Plate
15   How Do Protein Foods Help?
19   Dig into a Healthy Diet!

22   Glossary
23   Home and School Connection
24   Find Out More
24   Index

About the Author

Katie Marsico is an author of nonfiction books for children and young adults. She lives outside of Chicago, Illinois, with her husband and children.

What popular treat is made from chickpeas?

What Are Protein Foods?

What do you eat for lunch?

Do you like turkey? Maybe you prefer peanut butter. How about **hummus**?

These are all **protein** foods.

Proteins help your body's **cells** work. The foods you eat help your body make proteins.

Some protein foods come from animals. Meat and seafood are examples. So are **poultry** and eggs.

Other protein foods come from plants. This includes peas and beans. Nuts and seeds are also protein foods. So are some **soy products**.

Peas are special because they're both vegetables and protein foods.

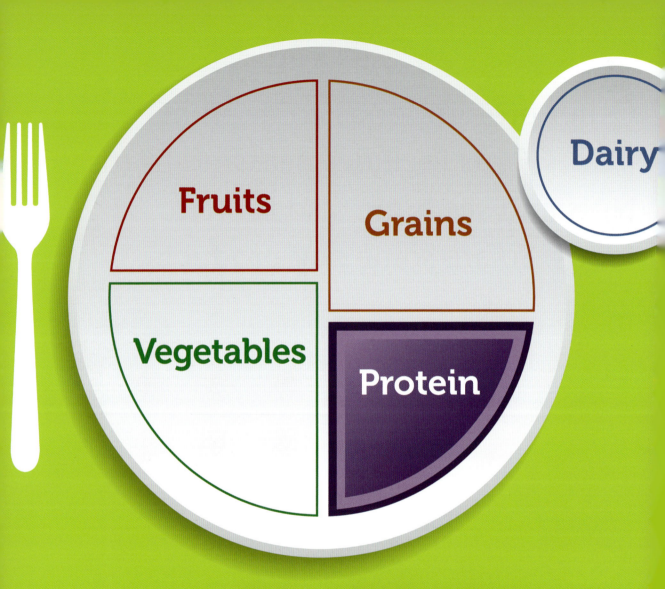

An Important Part of Your Plate

Protein foods are one of the five main **food groups**. These groups make up a **balanced diet**. You need each one to grow and stay strong.

How Do Protein Foods Help?

Proteins build bones and muscles. They also form skin and blood.

Protein foods have many **nutrients**. They help your body fight off illness. They keep your heart healthy too.

Dig into a Healthy Diet!

How much protein food do you need? You should have 4 to 5 ounces (.1 to .15 liter) daily.

Be sure to eat different foods. **Lean** meats are better for you.

Which protein foods will you eat next? Want to try something new? Make tasty, healthy choices!

Glossary

balanced diet (BAL-uhnsd DYE-it) eating just the right amounts of different foods

cells (SELZ) the tiniest units that make up living things

food groups (FOOD GROOPS) groups of different foods that people should have in their diet

hummus (HUH-muhs) a spread made from ground chickpeas and sesame seeds

lean (LEEN) having little fat

nutrients (NOO-tree-uhnts) substances that help you grow, stay energized, and keep alive

poultry (POL-tree) birds farmers raise for eggs or meat

products (PRAH-duhkts) things that are created and prepared for sale

protein (PROH-teen) a substance in certain foods that controls work done by your body's cells

soy (SOI) a plant in the pea family used to make foods such as tofu, soy milk, and tempeh

Home and School Connection

a	diet	includes	ounces	the
about	different	into	part	these
all	dig	is	peanut	they
also	do	keep	peas	they're
an	each	lean	plants	this
and	eat	like	plate	to
animals	eggs	lunch	popular	too
are	examples	made	poultry	treat
balanced	fight	main	prefer	try
be	five	make	products	turkey
beans	food	many	protein	up
because	for	maybe	seafood	vegetables
better	form	meat	seeds	want
blood	from	much	should	what
body	groups	muscles	skin	which
bones	grow	need	so	will
both	have	new	some	work
build	healthy	next	something	you
butter	heart	nutrients	soy	your
cells	help	nuts	special	
chickpeas	how	of	stay	
choices	hummus	off	strong	
come	illness	one	sure	
daily	important	other	tasty	

Find Out More

Book
Black, Vanessa. *Protein Foods*. Minneapolis, MN: Jump!, Inc., 2017.

Website
USDA—MyPlate Kids' Place
www.choosemyplate.gov/browse-by-audience/view-all-audiences/children/kids
Check out games and fast facts related to protein foods.

Index

animals, 9
beans, 11
cells, 7, 15
chickpeas, 4
diet, balanced, 13, 19–21
eggs, 9
food groups, 13
hummus, 5
meat, 9, 19
nutrients, 17
nuts, 11
peanut butter, 5
peas, 10, 11
plants, 11
poultry, 9
protein foods
 how much you should eat, 19
 how they help, 15–17
 what they are, 5–11
seafood, 9
seeds, 11
soy products, 11
turkey, 5